The Deep Woods

David Armand

The Deep Woods

David Armand

Blue Horse Press
P.O. Box 7000 - 760
Redondo Beach,
California   90277

Copyright © 2015 by David Armand.
All rights reserved.
Printed in the United States of America.

Cover art: "Abandoned Tracks of the Southern
Railroad, Moorhead, MS," by Jeffrey Alfier

Editors: Jeffrey and Tobi Alfier

ISBN   978-0692538142

Contents

Acknowledgments	vii
Mare Foaling in Winter	1
The Map	3
Hurt	5
Knife	8
Clair de Lune	12
Nostalgia	13
Cello	15
The Impressionist	17
A Deer's Death	18
Refraction	19
Night Terror	21
Early Morning in the Marsh	22
Photograph of My Father	24
Blood River, Springfield, Louisiana	26
The Deep Woods	28
About the Author	30

Acknowledgments

Grateful acknowledgment is made to the editors of the following journals in which some of these poems originally appeared, sometimes in slightly different form.

Calliope: "Refraction"

The Cape Rock: "A Deer's Death" and *"Clair de Lune"*

Eunoia Review: "Blood River, Springfield, Louisiana" and "Early Morning in the Marsh"

San Pedro River Review: "Night Terror"

The Texas Review: "The Deep Woods"

Town Creek Poetry: "Cello," "The Impressionist," "Knife," and "Hurt"

"Photograph of My Father" was selected by WRBH Reading Radio in New Orleans as the third place winner of their inaugural poetry competition. It is featured on their website, and was read by the author on air, which may be heard in its entirety at the following link: http://www.wrbh.org/wrbh-blog-poetry-contest-winners-meet-and-perform/
The author is grateful to the staff at the radio station, particularly David Benedetto, for letting him and his family tour the studio.

This book is dedicated to my children, Lily and Levi, with hopes these lines will remind them of how important family and memory are

Mare Foaling in Winter

Despite the cold the stall inside is warm.
It smells of dusty hay and lime,
the only light a single sixty watt bulb
hanging from an orange extension cord
which is stapled to a splintered rafter
and twists across the soffits like a snake.
The light fills the stall while outside
gray dawn comes cold and full
with winter's threat of sleet or even snow.

Inside the stall there's a father, a mother
and their three young children
surrounding a foaling brown mare.
They watch as she exhales warm breath
visible as smoke this winter morning
chuffing out from her large nostrils
her eyes worried and far-away discs
as her dusty withers twitch and pulse
sending a lethargic black fly alight.

The gnawed and serried boards around her
creak against the mare's sweat-streaked sides—
the giant hoops of her ribs and the life
inside of them pushing against the wall
as her whickering picks up and raises
the already-expectant pulse of everyone here.

They are all waiting.

The gray mud beneath them is soft
and cratered with the hoof prints
from the mare's carefully-shod hooves

and her many hours of pacing and stomping,
her halter clanging against her trough
as she scooped sweet feed into her mouth:
this same thing every day, but now she's giving
birth.
            The family huddles and watches
as first the tiny forelegs and head come forth
slick and white and alive but stuck.
Then the foal stops moving.
The mare's sides contract.
And now nothing—a quiet tableau.
And all inside the stall stands still.
Then the man stands up and grabs
a pair of metal calf-pullers which he soaked
earlier this morning in a tub of soapy water.
He uses them now to bring the foal into existence,
pulling as gently as he would a child
as though he had done this a hundred times.

The young family watches as the foal emerges.
It shakes its little head and breaks the sac
which had held it for some three hundred days.
It tries already to stand on its spindling legs
nudging toward its exhausted mother for milk.

The man puts down the calf-pullers now,
setting them on the ground in a bed of hay
and beside the rest of his tack and tools.
Then he goes over to sit with his family
to watch this new life nursing, breathing
waking to the promise of what's to follow.

The Map

I didn't know exactly where I was,
but the town of Waveland, Mississippi, is small
so I wasn't too worried when I rode over some train tracks
and wound up on a sandy asphalt road
that stretched along the Gulf Coast
like a plumb line laid flat all the way to Bay St. Louis.

I turned around, stopped at a convenience store
whose gas pumps had yellow tape around them
that said OUT OF SERVICE, but the store itself
was still open—a sign for ICE, BEER, MILK, BREAD
lit up behind the smudged glass and flickering
or faded in the places where the Freon had burned out.

I went inside and picked up a map from off the counter,
paid for it, then brought it back out to my car,
unfolding the giant page against the steering wheel.
I looked for where I was among the sprawling lines
(right next to the train tracks at this gas station here)
and then I traced with my finger to where I was trying to go:

Coral Street was on the other side of Highway 90, it said,
just down Waveland Avenue and then off Avenue B,
buried among a patch of woods and manmade canals.
I folded the map into a more manageable size,
put it on the empty passenger seat so I could still see
the roads I'd need to take to get from here to there.

It took me about ten minutes to get to the gravel road.
It was walled in on either side by pines, their boles
grayed by the dust chuffing out
from underneath my car's slowing tires,

crunching the rocks like tumbrel wheels
carrying me on some dark but necessary journey.

And then I stopped.
                    The map still sat on the seat,
one of its corners furling in on itself
as I looked out the window to my right,
where just behind a chest-high fence—
whose boards were warped and where poison ivy
grew through its slats like wires in an unfinished house—
a small camper sat. Its windows were boarded up
with sheets of moldy, chalk-marked plywood,
and a rusted-out truck was parked beside it.

There was a naked lightbulb just above the front door.
It was on. Someone was inside, in the dark, encapsulated
by the smell of mold and God-knows-what else,
just waiting there for the day that I would show up
like this. But I couldn't get out the car.
All I could do was sit there, the engine starting
to get overheated, the gauge moving slowly to *H*
like a finger wiping off a mistake on a chalkboard.

I was fifteen years old, couldn't fold a map,
couldn't even buy a pack of cigarettes
without a fake ID, and yet here I was
sitting in my car in front of the dilapidated trailer
where my mother lived.
                    My mother.
Whom I hadn't seen in a dozen years
and wouldn't see for a dozen more,
when I would be a father myself
and would remember that run-down camper
as I left it in a cloud of gray and lonely dust.

Hurt

My son was riding his bike
in the street yesterday
when he turned too sharp
fell down
and knocked out two of his teeth
against the cracked asphalt.

The blood was something to behold
coming out through his fingers
like that
as he ran toward me, crying
stumbling across the yard
in has damp and muddy socks.

We put him in the car and drove
to the Emergency Room
but after almost three hours
without seeing a doctor
we left.
        It was getting too late.

My son was feeling better by then
though his lip was swollen
and his chin and hands were scraped up
as though someone had taken
a stub of sandpaper to them.

His white school shirt
had turned pink at the collar
where the blood and spit
had leaked from the throbbing sockets
in his gums

where his beautiful white teeth had been
but now were gone
lying somewhere by the ditch
beside our driveway.

That night as I tried to sleep
I fell into a dream
in which I was building a house.
It reached up to the sky
like a cathedral, that house,
but when I stepped back
to see the work I'd done
it all started to come down
raining split soffits and bricks
all the dust and splinters now a thick cloud
bubbling up on the ground
around my feet.

My kids were there
and we were running now:
my daughter in my arms
crying something about her shoes—
that everything we had was gone.

And then I woke up.

I looked over at my two beautiful children
who were sleeping quietly
and I pulled the blanket over their legs
tried to fall back asleep myself.
But it was useless.
So I got out of bed.

It was still dark while I made the coffee

then sat on the sofa and pet the dog
watching the news on mute
so as not to wake anyone up.

Rain all day, it showed,
the splotches on the radar
green and yellow and even red
in spots, moving across Louisiana
like someone dragging a sheet
over a field for a picnic.

This was fine by me:
I was taking off work anyway.
I needed to be home for a while.

Knife

My dad kept a shoebox full of knives
in his closet next to several boxes
of shotgun shells and his .38 revolver—
it was all on a top shelf
and out of our reach.

Sometimes he would take it down
for us to look at
since some of the knives in that box were mine
or otherwise my brother's.

We each had a Swiss Army knife in there
which held a small blade
tweezers, a nail file, scissors
and a little plastic toothpick
you could pull out of that glossy red handle
with your fingernail.

Then there were two folding knives
with varnished beechwood handles
where our initials
had been engraved with a woodburning tool
its orange metal tip smoldering
until there was a dark brown *D.A.* on mine
and a *B.A.* on my brother's.

But my favorite knife was one
I got at the parish fair one night
as we were walking down
the dusty, haystrewn midway
my dad in front of us
his faded brown boots

stepping over myriad rills
of spilled drinks
cigarette butts and Coke cups
over endless yards
of orange and black extension cords
through which all the power flowed
lighting up the drooping strands of bulbs overhead
and the yellow and red ones on the Ferris wheel
and the many blinking lights
on the Gravitron, the Scrambler, the bumper cars—
all encircled by metal barricades
and lines of people waiting in the balding grass
to get on, the tips of their cigarettes glowing
like lightning bugs.

                As we walked by
there were grizzled men in booths
calling out to us from behind a scrim
of neon-lit cigarette smoke
the smell of funnel cakes
                      cotton candy
                                popcorn
                                          livestock
telling everyone to take a chance:
one dollar one try
three dollars five tries.

You could win it all, they said.
Stuffed animals, posters
a balsawood plane you launched
with a rubber band.

But my dad ignored them
pitching his own cigarette

into the dust
and we kept walking

stopping only when we saw some knives
hanging from a sheet of pocked corkboard
in one of the painted wooden booths.
These were Bowie knives, he told us
and he wanted my brother and me
each to have one.

                    It was important, he said
that we each had some good knives
in our collection
and that we knew how to use them
to revere them for their power
and what they could do to you
if you weren't careful
(he had been stabbed when he was a kid
playing around with a switchblade—
the one with the pearl handle
that he still kept in the shoebox
in his closet next to ours).

Then he bought us each one of the knives
from that carnival barker
handing us the little box they came in
and he let us keep them clipped
to our belts for the rest of the night
though later they would end up in that shoe-
box with the others, only to be seen
every once in a while.

Lord, I can still remember
that knife's black leather sheath

how it was cracked and faded
around the edges
how it snapped shut
over the brass crosspiece
to keep the blade from slipping out.

I remember the way the wood handle
felt in my hand—the heft of it—
how the blade sounded when you slid
it out the sheath
                and when you put it back in.

Now that my dad's been gone
some fifteen years, if you can believe it,
I wish I still had that knife
wish I knew what happened
to that shoebox it was in
if for no other reason
so that I could show it to my kids one day—
keep it on a shelf in the closet
hidden in a shoebox, like my dad did—
until they are old enough and ready
to understand its significance.

Clair de Lune

This is a memory I do not have:
sitting side by side on a rickety piano bench
my legs too short to reach the floor
      (since I'm just a boy)
as you play *Clair de Lune* for me
your fingers carefully pressing out each note:
the sharps, the flats, those soft impressionistic chords.
When you're done, you bend to kiss
me on the head. You tell me that you love me.
I'm the only son you would ever have.

How I do remember you, though, is like this:
finding you on the floor of your trailer
the bottle of Librium beside you open
half of them gone, the rest strewn
across the linoleum like black-and-baby-blue gravel
culled from the bottom of a dirty fish tank
your shallow, staccato breath
barely coming through your half-opened mouth
as though filled with wads of cotton
unable to say a word.

Nostalgia

Going back to the land where I grew up
fishing through a box of old photographs
to give to my mother on her birthday
I find a picture of myself as a boy:
a Remington .410 Wingmaster in one hand
three or four dead bobwhites in the other.

I put the picture in my back pocket
decide to keep this one for myself
I can't exactly tell you why
and then I take my wife and kids outside
where we climb on one of the four wheelers
and ride down the horse trails in the woods.

We drive over steep clay banks and muddy swales
and into the shade of the pine thickets
which still surround the patch of land
where I was raised among what's wild
my hair blowing back in the wind
as we pass horses, deer stands
large brown rabbits, a hawk. And I show
my kids these things they never get to see.

We pass by my whole life, it seems
spooling out before us like jute twine
never long enough to reach the end of the road
and then, before we know it, we're back
in the clearing where we started off.

They used to say nostalgia was a disease
literally a sickness for the past or home
but I like to think that instead of being sick

I simply long to be the boy I was
so as to better pass on this world
to my children. I'm telling you
I want my kids to carry this with them
in their own lives, down their own roads
which even though they lead away from home
they're always returning, always coming back.

Cello

The moment before the strings suddenly snapped
free from his instrument's smoothed surface
sending the sound of a shotgun blast
out from the pulpit and over the pews
outside, down the pigeon-cowled stairway
of the St. Louis Cathedral at morning mass
the boy behind the cello had his eyes closed
and was thinking of the time he got lost
in a corn field as a child,

                        walking down
the rows and rows and kicking at the stalks
his three feet two inches a third the size
of the swaying stems: a maze of yellow-brown
surrounding him on every side but up

where the sky was blue, clear blue, and cold
but as the boy looked there and saw it getting dark
he ran the way he thought he knew was home
until it all began to look the same—
the stalks like living light poles on each side
confusing him, like the things around us do
when we're young and scared and can hardly tell
the ground from rows of corn or evening sky—
and he started to call for his father, who broke
his way through the stalks until he was there

scooping his son up in his farm-hardened arms
and then held him snug against his warm work shirt
telling him, "I'm here, stop crying, I'm here"
as if this was all that needed to be said

so that when the boy opened his eyes, he was back
in the cathedral and could see his father now
sitting in the pews with everybody else
not owing a thought to anything but faith—
faith his son would be okay, that this, like time
would pass and the noise of those broken strings
would fade away into the sanctuary
while the orchestra picked up where it left off

and the boy put down his bow and just listened then
as if nothing bad had ever happened to him.

The Impressionist

The low-green light from the console
stretching over your face, hands, body,
windows cracked to let the smoke out—
some cheap pot's all it takes to turn
my head into a landscape of memories
like I'm blurred across a canvas
of one of those French painters—
Impressionists, I think they're called.

I slept through most of Art History,
but I remember two or three slides
clicking through the projector's wheel
like gears locking home in a new tranny—
a sound I dream about, would pay to hear
even if I didn't give a damn about cars
couldn't rebuild an engine in forty hours flat
or trace a leak in a fuel line.

Those foggy landscapes, smeared-on skies,
smiling waitresses in a fuzzy café,
stuff I never really understood, much less
cared about. But right now, with the radio
hovering over our voices, and the engine's hum
almost visible through the windshield,
your arms are soft and illuminated like candles
keeping my eyes open, waiting for that next click.

A Deer's Death

A trail of upturned mud left in the grass
and several small trees that had been cracked
in half or smashed along the narrow path,
and pulled-down power lines like rubber bands
were all I had to understand the sight
I saw through my windshield, blurred and foggy
as it was with the rain that still poured down,
but it was certainly enough for me
to figure out what nature must've done
to bring so many people out of bed
like witnesses to some great tragedy
or the unlikely bearers of a weight
that rested in ballooning, rain-drenched flesh
discarded in the grass when those swift winds
came snake-like from the clouds, and rumbling,
swept up the little doe from her wandering
over the dewy leaves and grass she ate
and spun her left and right 'til life left her,
spitting her out like something that went stale,
all the stuff that made it good now gone.

Refraction

A cold front blew through last night
bringing with it gusting swales
of wind and rain
which must've knocked the power out
while we were still asleep in bed.

The blinking red numbers
on the digital clock said 3AM,
though I don't think that was right.
Yet I got up from bed and stumbled
into the dark kitchen for a glass of water.

Then I cut the alarm, let the dog out,
and even though it's over a mile
away from here, I could hear a train
howling and screeching across the tracks
all the way from my front door.

It must have been the colder, thinner air
that helped the sound to make its way this far.
Refraction, I think it's called.
It was the only thing I could think of
as I stared at the spackling of stars overhead.

I imagined those damp gray cars,
could almost see them tattooed
with their bright graffiti, barreling past,
and that long, long trail of freighters and tanks,
all of it sliding quickly through the dark.

I heard the train's loud horn bellowing,
the metal on metal as it skirled

over the tracks. And I'm imagining this, too:
the wheels shooting up blue-white sparks
as the train heads north into Mississippi.

Night Terror

I hate bridges, and in my dreams
I'm always going over one
a black narrow line stretching
up into the vast, cloud-filled sky
like God's dark finger reaching down
and touching the road in front of the car.

I try to turn around but can't,
my ears popping now with the altitude
and when I finally reach the summit
I can see over the metal guardrail
the angry, roiling water beating
against the pylons, which are always
twined with metal stairs, leading
up (or down) like strands of DNA.

People are usually going over these steps
moving slowly and with blank faces
most of them falling somehow
only to be sliced in two by the myriad cables
that are holding up the bridge.

Then *I* go over—either in my car
or after having jumped—
all the air in my lungs sucked out
as I wake up finally
screaming and gasping for breath.

Early Morning in the Marsh

After we toss the black plastic decoys
we paddle out across the marsh
the gray horizon giving way to orange
as the sun wheels up above the reeds.

Their stalks are black silhouettes
against the cold, early-morning sky
as a vee of ducks scatters in the distance.

The oars scrape the sides of the pirogue
as it sways toward the duck-blind
and noses up against a muddy finger of earth.

Then we climb out as the mud and water suck
at our waders. You haul our shotguns
into the blind and straighten out the reeds
which are laced through sheets of chicken-wire
and stapled onto a frame of damp two by fours.

You say this should be good enough for now.

Then I watch you take the wooden duck call
from the frayed lanyard around your neck
and blow into it. We both wait and watch
the mallards, blue-winged teal, widgeon,
wood ducks and canvasbacks skim by overhead.

You raise your .12 gauge to your shoulder
and pick off a duck with each of your three shots.
The smell of gunpowder climbs into my nose
as the dead birds pirouette from the sky.

I watch you eject the smoking plastic shells
into the tall grass beside our blind
then look off into the distance and watch
the rest of the ducks fly away
like a handful of tossed gravel—
a missed opportunity.

Photograph of My Father

> *All his life my father wanted to be bold.*
> —Raymond Carver

You're standing in the kitchen of that old trailer
that you rented for us on Davidson Road
and where we lived for a couple of months
while you cleared some land just north of here in Folsom
to put another trailer that you were going to buy new.

I remember that one of the toilets in that old place
never flushed right and the whole trailer leaned
on its cinder blocks so that all the doors inside
hung wrong and they would creak open
in the middle of the night sometimes.

But there was a horse paddock in the front yard,
a couple of stalls where once I watched
you help deliver a colt and where another time
I saw you get kicked in the chest by its father.

There was also a great field where we rode Go-Karts
and where one time you pulled my brother and me
behind your truck on our scooters
with a piece of rope you found in the shed.

We hunted quail back there in that field too,
pitched baseballs, shot bows and arrows
at little paper targets. And we went fishing
in a pond that was on another man's land.

That's where you caught the fish you're holding
in this picture. It's a bass that for some reason

you called "Walter." Its silver scales and wide mouth
are open around your closed hand and its caudal fin
comes all the way down to your belt—
I swear that fish must've been three feet long.

You're smiling about as much as you ever did here:
your teeth aren't showing. Just a tight, hard grin
that's barely visible beneath your beard
and your beer-reddened face and cheeks.

You're also younger in this picture
than I am now, probably by at least five years,
and have only a dozen more left to live.
But of course you don't know that here.
How could you?

Behind you the counter's covered with grocery bags,
a box of Frosted Flakes, some pots and pans
and their lids. There's a sugar bowl, paper towels
a couple of two liter bottles of Coke, a coffee maker.

You're standing in front of that counter
and just to the right of a dingy yellow refrigerator
wearing dark jeans and green hospital scrubs
that you got when you went to the Emergency Room
after you nailed your hand to a rabbit cage that time.
Do you remember that?

Anyway, this fish you're holding is staring out
past your thick, dark arms, past the mess
of our kitchen and the mess of the life you built
for us but that was still somehow pretty good.

Blood River, Springfield, Louisiana

I'm hauling the boat I just bought last summer
behind my little pick-up truck down Highway 22
my wife and kids behind me in her van
when I turn off onto a muddy gravel road
leading to a boat launch on the Tickfaw River.

Since my father never taught me how to drive a boat
much less launch one into a body of water
its dark embrace enveloping that smooth hull
as if it's falling into a pile of cool bedsheets,
I have to rely on what here in Louisiana
would be considered simple common sense
though this is not so simple or common at all to me.

My foot quivers on the clutch as I back up
to where the gravel road ends at a concrete ramp
over which two people can back their trailers in at once
side-by-side, and then ease their boats into the river.
I pull the parking brake once my trailer's submerged,
get out my truck and walk knee-deep into the oily water.
Then I turn the winch until the boat is free
and I can pull it by its soaking hawser
to one of the pilings at the edge of the dock.

You see, I was born and raised here
out in the country up around Folsom
if you want to get specific about it
but I missed out on some of the best parts
since my dad was always too drunk
or too busy or just too damned angry
to show me how to do these things himself:
like boating, fishing, how to skin a deer.

I tie the boat off so I can park my truck
and meet my family in the weeded lot
grab the life jackets and help drag the ice chest
which is packed with sandwiches my wife made
chips, and a tiny passel of Cokes and beers.

And here I am trying to make up for my past
by showing my kids these things
that I don't even really know myself

and I wonder if my dad would be proud of me
for taking my family out on the water
like he always talked about doing, but never did.

We climb in the boat and head toward the Blood River
the wind blowing my kids' hair back as we speed up
and the channel widens, spooling out before us
before it splits and curves into a nice shaded spot
where we drop the anchor and jump into the water:
the river's warm with patches of cold
that wrap around your legs and chest
and every now and then you can feel a fish glide by.

This is new to all of us, but I swear
it's as though we've done it a thousand times—
since I was a kid myself.

The Deep Woods

> *And miles to go before I sleep.*
> —Robert Frost

See the boy. He is alone in a dark clearing.
He's surrounded by gray pines, webbed
together with deadfall and thick smoke
which is coming off his dying fire
like heavy fog over a morning lake.
The fire's black remnants lie smoldering
on a hard patch of earth before him.

The ground is damp at the boy's feet
and he sips from a dented canteen
the last of his water
tinged the color of cardboard
from the tannins in the ditch
where he had sloshed it up
just before he stopped here to rest.

And now he sits beside the trail. It twists
through the woods like a snake's intestines
and leads to where he'd been told
his father lives in a rundown shack.
This is where he plans to meet this man
though he never claimed the boy as his.
But he has made a promise, in theory,
that the boy thinks the man should keep.

He's been out here for days, this boy,
braving the cold, the rain, the darkness
all bearing down on him at once
the only warmth the thought

of sharing a good meal with his father:
venison, maybe sweet potatoes
burnt black around the edges
over a scullery fire, its flame
as orange as the soft meat
that oozes out the skin like molten slag.

Now see the boy get up
start once again for the crooked path
which will take him to where he wants to go.
But first watch him stop to let a deer leap
from out of a copse and then disappear
its black eye a marble
shot into a sun-bleached two by four
reflecting nothing behind it
and looking only at what's ahead.

About the Author

David Armand was born and raised in Louisiana. He has worked as a drywall hanger, a draftsman, and as a press operator in a flag printing factory. He now teaches at Southeastern Louisiana University, where he also serves as associate editor for Louisiana Literature Press. In 2010, he won the George Garrett Fiction Prize for his first novel, *The Pugilist's Wife*, which was published by Texas Review Press. His second novel, *Harlow*, was published by Texas Review Press in 2013. David's third novel, *The Gorge*, is forthcoming this fall from Southeast Missouri State University Press; and his memoir, *My Mother's House*, is forthcoming Spring 2016 from Texas Review Press. David lives with his wife and two children and is working on his sixth book, *The Lord's Acre*.

www.ingramcontent.com/pod-product-compliance
Lightning Source LLC
Chambersburg PA
CBHW031508040426
42444CB00007B/1256